You Have a Voice

By Marie Pflugrad

Illustrated by Kevin Jones

Copyright © 2020 Marie Pflugrad
Copyright © 2020 TEACH Services, Inc.
ISBN-13: 978-1-4796-1180-5 (Paperback)
ISBN-13: 978-1-4796-1181-2 (ePub)
Library of Congress Control No: 2020913415

TEACH Services, Inc.
PUBLISHING
www.TEACHServices.com • (800) 367-1844

Introduction

As a retired schoolteacher, Marie Pflugrad is passionate about children and education. Her upbringing in the mountains of Colorado have given her a love of both nature and animals. After healing and recovery from childhood abuse and trauma, Marie was inspired to combine these two passions to write this book. "It's ironic that while many animals have a built-in form of self-defense, children don't, or do they?" Marie uses her woodland puppets to help children recognize that they do have a means by which they can protect themselves.

The goal for this book, *You Have a Voice*, is not only to bring awareness to the epidemic of childhood sexual abuse, but it is to be used as a preventative tool. While **stranger danger** has been taught, and most children are aware of what to do in the event of an attempted abduction by a stranger, there isn't a lot of awareness about the abuses that take place by those we **do** know. It is the goal of this author to make this book available to any and all people and organizations who spend time with children in any capacity. Education is critical, but it's not enough just to teach children to be resilient and self-assertive, they must be taught that it is okay to tell someone to STOP! It's okay to use their voice to tell when someone has done something to them. Children need to learn what "grooming" signs to watch for so they are not lured in by a "nice" person. This educational step is the first step to prevention!

As the author has experienced, it is much better to help a child when they are young than to try to repair years of repressed damage. Research proves that often a perpetrator was once

a victim themselves. Wouldn't prevention be a better solution than convicting a criminal who was once a victim? There has to be a way to stop this cycle of pain. Please allow Joetta, Spike, Shelley, and Squirt to share their stories to teach children that they indeed do have a voice.

Marie has a website where you can go to get more information and download free educational tools as well as statistics on this subject.

For more information and for warning signs of possible sexual abuse in a child's behavior please visit Marie's website at: www.youhaveavoice.org.

No sharp quills like a nail,
You can't hide in a shell
You don't make a smell
But You Have a Voice
So be brave and tell!!!

Joetta sat on the swing on the front porch of her cozy, little yellow house. It was a sunny April morning and she drank her cup of warm tea as she watched the neighbor children play in the front yard. Lacey was four years old and her brother Logan was seven. "What sweet children," Joetta thought to herself.

Suddenly the *screeeeech* of the brakes on the bus startled Joetta and she realized it was time to get ready for work. Logan rolled the ball to Lacey one more time as he headed for the bus. Lacey and her mom waved good-bye to Logan as the bus slowly pulled away to go to school. Joetta went inside and packed her special work bags and prepared to leave her cozy, little yellow house for her wonderful job. Joetta was a counselor. She helped people when they had problems and needed someone to talk to. Sometimes she even talked to children. Children can have problems, too.

"Good morning children! My name is Joetta and I am so glad to be here with you today!"

Joetta was a very nice, tall lady who wore black pants with a green sweater. Her hair was pulled back in a long braid and she had wire-rimmed glasses. She carried a big brown bag that was full and lumpy. The children were excited to have a guest speaker in class today. They didn't know what she was going to talk about, but they looked forward to not having to do their schoolwork … at least for a little while.

Mrs. Scott, the teacher, instructed the students to form a half-circle on the carpet while Joetta joined them and sat in the overstuffed bean bag chair in front of the boys and girls.

Joetta gathered the students around her. First, she talked to the children about something they already knew. "How many of you know what "stranger danger" means?" Joetta asked.

Aubrey's hand went up immediately. "It's what I'm supposed to yell if someone I don't know tries to grab me!" Aubrey exclaimed.

"Very good. That is exactly right," Joetta said. "What I want to talk to you about today is very important. It is similar to "stranger danger" except that sometimes someone might want to hurt us or do something bad to us, and we *do* know them. Some people are not strangers at all."

Joetta had a gentle look on her face as she talked to the children.

"I don't want to scare you." Joetta continued. "I just want to make sure you know that sometimes bad things can happen to us and some of you might already know what I'm talking about." Joetta continued, "Students, sometimes, there might be a person you know who tries to talk you into letting them touch you in ways that don't feel good. They might even ask you to touch their body in places you don't want to touch." Joetta paused. "Have any of your parents talked to you about this?" Joetta asked. Billy, Ronnie, and Becky slowly poked their hands up. "Thank you," Joetta said. "You can put your hands down. I'm glad some of your parents have talked to you."

Joetta could see the wide eyes of the children as they leaned in and listened to every word she had to say.

Joetta pulled a fuzzy object out of her bag. "I'd like you to meet Spike," Joetta smiled. "He is my porcupine friend and he would like to share a story with you."

Joetta had slipped the brown puppet over her hand and in a slightly different voice, Spike introduced himself. "Hello boys and girls! My name is Spike and I am a porcupine. I would like to tell you a story about a time when I went camping with some friends. One of the older boys was very nice to me. He gave me some of his candy and shared things with me. I thought he liked me, and I thought he was my friend. But when we were camping, he told me he wanted to touch me, and he tried! But I puffed up and I poked out my very sharp quills. "STOP!" I yelled. "This is my body, not yours, and only I can touch my body. Don't you come any closer!"

Spike sighed and said, "The older boy left me alone and I was safe. I'm so glad I can protect myself. You may not have sharp quills like I have, **but you have a voice**. You need to talk to someone you trust, even if the person tells you not to. Don't be afraid to yell STOP! if someone tries to hurt you. Thank you, boys and girls, for listening to my story."

Joetta placed Spike back in her oversized bag and asked the students if they understood what Spike told them. Little heads nodded up and down. "Are there any questions?" Joetta asked.

"What else do you have in the bag?" Lonnie smiled curiously.

"I'm glad you asked," said Joetta. "I'd like to introduce you to another friend of mine."

Joetta slowly pulled out a shy, green turtle. "Boys and girls, this is Shelley, and she is very shy. Shelley asked me to talk to you and to tell you that she also had someone who tried to hurt her." Joetta went on, "Shelley had a relative that came to visit her house several times. The relative wanted to see Shelley without her shell on, but Shelley didn't feel comfortable about it."

Suddenly, Shelley poked her head out of her shell and looked down at the children and in a timid, but hopeful voice, she said "Boys and girls, I have a shell that I can hide in. I'm very glad that my shell protected me when I needed it, and I was safe from my relative." Shelley sighed, "But I know you don't have a shell to hide in, **but you have a voice**. Please don't be shy like I was. I was afraid and too scared to tell anyone." Shelley poked her head back in her shell and Joetta slowly placed Shelley back in the big bag.

"What would you do if you were Shelley?" Joetta thoughtfully asked the boys and girls.

Lots of little hands went up. Maya couldn't contain herself, "I would tell my mom and dad!" she blurted out. "Me too!" several little voices said at the same time.

"I hope so; I hope you would all be brave and find someone you could talk to that you trust," said Joetta. "Remember what Spike and Shelley said, '**You have a voice.**'"

"I have one more friend I want you to meet," smiled Joetta. "Her name is April, but her friends and family call her Squirt." Out of the bag popped a black and white striped … skunk. The children burst into laughter. "I bet you know how I defend myself," April said as the children calmed back down. "My mom and dad told me that I am only to use my spray when I am in real danger." April had a sad look on her face and her head went down toward the floor.

"I was at my church for Vacation Bible School. Church is supposed to be a safe place to be, I thought," said April. "But someone at the church that I knew and trusted stopped me and grabbed me, and started touching me. I was so scared; I couldn't help myself and I sprayed." April looked embarrassed. "I tried to tell my mom and dad when they came to pick me up, but they wouldn't listen to me. It made me sad and mad." April looked a little feisty now, and she bristled up her fuzzy tail. "Boys and girls, I know you can't spray someone who is trying to hurt you, **but you have a voice** and you can scream. You can tell your mom and dad. If they don't believe you, then you need to find someone else who will listen to you." April was calming down now, and she put her fuzzy tail down. "No one should touch you in ways that make you feel yucky. You deserve to be safe and I hope you will remember my story. You can call me Squirt if you want to."

"Do you believe Squirt?" Joetta asked the class.

"Yes!" shouted the entire class.

"Do you think Squirt told someone else?" Joetta waited as the children thought about the question.

Again, "yes" answers started being shouted.

"Do you think you could be brave like Squirt and tell someone if this happened to you?" Nods of "yes" and little voices agreeing followed. Joetta then placed Squirt back in her big bag.

"You do have voices, boys and girls," Joetta said. "Even here at school, if you are afraid of a bully or if someone tries to touch you inappropriately in the bathroom, or in the locker room, or even at recess, or anywhere, please find someone to tell if you are scared of someone and feel like you could be hurt. Even if you know the person. Even if they are not a stranger. Even if they live right in your own house. Please tell someone you can trust!"

Joetta packed her things and gave each of the students a keepsake reminder that read: **YOU HAVE A VOICE**.

Before she left the classroom, Joetta spoke with Mrs. Scott. "Mrs. Scott, some of your students may want to share their own stories with you. Please call me if you would like my help."

As Joetta was leaving, Mrs. Scott asked the students to thank Joetta for coming today. "Thank you, Joetta!" shouted the students in unison. And applause erupted in the classroom.

As Joetta drove home, she could still see the innocent faces of Mrs. Scott's students. Oh, how she hoped she could make a difference in their lives. As she pulled into her driveway, the bus was just stopping in front of Logan and Lacey's house. Logan ran up the sidewalk and greeted his little sister who was waiting for him to get home. Joetta whispered a silent prayer, "Please protect these innocent little children. Please don't let anyone hurt them." Joetta waved at Logan and Lacey and their mom and went into her cozy, little yellow house. She had a wonderful day teaching the children that they indeed do have a voice.

www.TEACHServices.com • (800) 367-1844

We invite you to view the complete
selection of titles we publish at:
www.TEACHServices.com

We encourage you to write us
with your thoughts about this,
or any other book we publish at:
info@TEACHServices.com

TEACH Services' titles may be purchased in
bulk quantities for educational, fund-raising,
business, or promotional use.
bulksales@TEACHServices.com

Finally, if you are interested in seeing
your own book in print, please contact us at:
publishing@TEACHServices.com

We are happy to review your manuscript at no charge.

www.ingramcontent.com/pod-product-compliance
Lightning Source LLC
Chambersburg PA
CBHW061119170426
43200CB00023B/3000